Words - Words - Words

Jack Killester

BookLeaf
Publishing

Presentation by *BookLeaf Publishing*

Web: www.bookleafpub.com

E-mail: info@bookleafpub.com

ISBN: 9789357441605

First edition 2023

DEDICATION

To all who fill the world with words.

ACKNOWLEDGEMENT

To my family.
K, H and E - You are my everything.
Mum - For everything you have done and do.

PREFACE

Challenged to produce three weeks worth of poems, Jack Killester churned out a series of creativity which surprised him... and which he vowed never to do it again! Being put under the literary cosh was a challenge which he achieved in the same way that a dentist extracts a collapsed root canal. Enjoy.

A Fresh Start

My New Year's Resolutions

- Identify two Rubik's cubes solutions
- Spend less time in the shower = reduce
ablutions
- Donate more to charity =increase contributions
- I MUST cut back on my petrol pollution
by buying a Tesla (chance of electrocution?)
- Witness state sponsored murders = (2
executions?)
- Add more water to cordial - improved dilutions
- Assist military coups = instigate revolutions
-Support Indy Ref 2 = Ensure Scot's
devolutions!
- Avenge injured innocents = seek retribution
- Study ancient philosophies (Stoicism?
Confucian?)
-Plead with the pope = request absolution

...Stop wasting my life making lists!!!

An Ode to a Year 10 Classroom

By the veins within my temple you can see that I am
stressing,
Like I am stood before the firing squad and
desperately confessing.

You're pushing me to breakdown
with your talking and your messin'
For a moment please be quiet,
I just want to teach this lesson!

I can scream, berate or upbraid till my face is beetroot
puce,
But that's a pathetic little whimper to the noise you
can produce.
The very pit of hell is like a softly babbling brook,
Our classroom's pandemonium,
please just open up your book!!

I've spent so long stood screaming,
I've developed bad sciatica,
I have constant crushing migraines
from inhaling your Lynx Africa.
Your stench is rampant hormones, Vosene shampoo,
unbrushed teeth.
It's mephitic, it is noxious, it is quite beyond belief.

I'm stood begging for your interest,
Your attention I'm imploring,
Yes I know that what I'm teaching is irrelevant and
boring.
You balance your new mobile on your lap beneath the
desk
Your greasy, dandruff hairdo is disgustingly grotesque.

The thing that's most depressing is I once sat in your
seat,
I was apathy incarnate I thought school was obsolete.
Until three weeks 'fore I finished when at last the
penny dropped
When I took Jane Smith the movies and my debit card
was stopped.

My God the shame! The cringing! I was absolutely
brassic!
I never got to see the park that had dinosaurs Jurassic.
Instead Jane used a ten pence piece, called her Dad to
pick her up.
I was about as well respected as the Uefa Super Cup.

Now I know that when you look at me you see a
washed up teacher,
And with all my best intentions it's unlikely that I'll
reach yer,(sic)
With my ratty beard and my coffee breath,
My wrinkled skin and stench of death.

But PLEASE just take a minute, stamp the brakes on,
have a think!

Don't wait til the last minute when your dreams are
down the sink.
If you carry on and fail,
if you sit the test and lose,
...then in another thirty years you could be stood
inside my shoes!

New Beginnings

Return to work,
The end of Christmas,
Scowl returning,
Back to business.

Endless meetings,
Pointless nonsense,
Nodding yes men,
Correspondance.

Empty staplers,
Out of office,
Fake reunions,
Feeling nauseous.

Chucking dead plants,
Fantasising,
Completing spreadsheets,
Analysing.

Goodwill crumbling,
Cheer forgotten,
Stench from top drawer,
Something's rotten.

12 more months,
Til Christmas presents.
Kind to others?
Evanescence.

I Just Want to Think About You

I don't want to think about money,
I don't want to discuss the rent
I don't want to talk 'bout the gas bill,
Or the fact I can't put up a tent.

I don't want to scrub at the dishes,
Or chat 'bout the shortage of bread,
I don't want to take out the bin bags
But there's something I will do instead.

I don't want to visit your mother,
I don't want to go to the zoo,
I don't want to think of another,
I just want to think about you.

The Creature of Driffin.

Slanting beams of a dying light,
The soft caress of breeze,
The swift approach of an autumn night,
The screech of twisting keys.

For in the town of Driffen,
The sun dispels all fears,
But in the night near Driffen,
No-one's ventured out in years.

A creature prowls through Driffen,
Spoken of in secret tones,
It drinks the blood of innocents
Sucks marrow from their bones.

Its kiss is always deadly
Climbs through windows,
Bursts through doors.
Attacks the town of Driffen
Dragging children to the moors.

If you travel down to Driffen,
If you choose to stay the night,
Be sure to take precautions,
And don't turn out the light.

Someday I'll Dive Again

The waves surge in and I am back in its grip.
When the tide pulled at me like a scorned lover.
My lungs and resolve compressing,
And letting me sink into the freezing warmth of
the deep.
Through the veil of the waves I could glimpse
the dimming stars,
And I nearly slipped from myself.

Missing a breath, a heartbeat, a stroke.
And my life didn't flash before my eyes,
And I remember thinking it was a con!
Maybe I hadn't done enough to be reminded of.
Bastard memory!
It's been leaving me in the lurch for years.

That missed anniversary.
My desk drawer passport.

But I can remember gasping in the ocean,

I don't know what spurred me on to make one
last attempt for the shore.
Maybe it was the thought of washing up on an
unfamiliar beach?

Yet I don't get scared on the beach now,
Even though the waves smile at me
And urge me to come back
To oblivion.
I am sure I will one day.
Someday I'll dive again.

Grow Old Again

Waking in an unfamiliar bed
A strange new head on my shoulder
An invigorating perfume
An unusual scent on the sheet.

I think of my wife at home
The ease with which she swallowed the lie.
"I'm at a friends",
"A Conference",
"A late shift",
The relief with which she received it,
Anything but the truth.

I'd forgotten how lust could be so powerful
All consuming and ferocious.
A satiated, hushed conversation.
Inches apart.

I had forgotten,
This delicious explosion
Of youth.
Must return soon to the past.
And grow old again.

Grandad Ron

My Granddad Ron LOVED to play hide and
seek.
We would play it for hours, at least once a week.
He would always play properly, always count up
to ten.
We would search for each other again and again.

He would always find somewhere AMAZING to
hide,
Sometimes up on the shed,
Sometimes under the slide,
One time I found him,
buried deep in a hedge
And once in his garden, concealed by his veg!
Once in the shower,
Once in the bin!
He loved it so much, and he wanted to win!

One day I went round and was ready to play,
But when I arrived Nan said
"Granddad's away."
He's been very poorly…
Your Granddad is gone...

Never again would I see Granddad Ron.

I wanted to cry so I wandered away,.
I sat in the garden where we used to play.
It was there that I saw it – hidden under the slide
A small piece of paper just where Ron used to
hide.

At the top of the sheet was a small number "1"
In the familiar scrawl of my old Granddad Ron!
I spotted another perched high up on the shed,
Another was left in the vegetable bed.
One in the shower,
And one in the hedge,
One in the bin, (sellotaped to the edge!)

Each small note was numbered so I put them in
order,
They were all from my Granddad with his name
in the border.

They said "Dearest Grandson, if you have these
I'm gone,
I won't say I am in heaven or I'm just moving
on,
No-one quite knows what happens,
after you're dead.
But my story's not over (the tiny notes said).

I live on in your memory,
when I hid in the hedge,
when I squashed in the bin and got stuck in the
veg.
when I crammed in the shower, crouched down
under the slide
And whenever your Grandson asks if you'll go
and hide,
Remember when we played, and don't feel too
upset.
I live on within you,
and never forget!
I am proud of you, love you, playing with you
was fun
You were one of my best friends my beloved
Grandson

The Lot Less Monster

The Lot Less Monster

Monsters from all around the world,
Often keep in touch online.
They talk about their sightings,
And make sure their mums are fine

There was Yeti. There was Bigfoot
There was Werewolf. There was Sphinx
There was a Labrador from Singapore
Who never, ever blinks

But by far the most well-known of them,
Was shrouded in deep water.
Here is Scotland's Loch Ness monster,
And her little, tiny daughter

Her daughter was a tiddler,
wouldn't come up to your knee.
She stayed out of the limelight,
Spent her time far out at sea.

Because she was so small her mum had named
her just "LOT LESS"

She was the "Lot less monster"
and she shared her mum's address.

When monster hunters visited,
She'd keep well out of view
Her mum would stretch out her long neck,
Like the bigger Nessie's do.

The Lot Less Monster tried this once.
Stuck her head up to the sky.
But a Scotsman thought she was a twig,
Which just made Lot Less cry.

She decided she would stay below,
Til she was fully grown.
But that all changed one winter's day,
Whilst mum was on the phone.

"Lot Less" heard her mum coughing,
It was clear that she was ill.
Her nose was red, her fins were limp,
She had a swollen gill.

Her Mum said to her Mummy friend,
 "I need to show my face,
If I don't, I'll let my fans down,
I'll be shrouded in disgrace."

Lot Less decided she would go

She'd take big Nessie's place.
She put on two bright armbands
And a grimace on her face

She swam up to the surface
And with a graceful "Splish"
Found dozens on the waterside.
She'd fulfil her mum's wish!

But before she could submerge herself,
An awful thing occurred.
The monster hunters laughed at her
She heard one say "Absurd!"

"Look at that little Nessie!
I've seen bigger loaves of bread!
I can't believe how cute it looks!"
The three main gawkers said.

"Cute!" Thought Little Lot Less.
How dare they think I'm cute!!
I'll show them who's adorable,
I'll leave them destitute!!

"Lot Less" breathed in her deepest breath,
Then let out a fearsome shriek.
The cameras shattered on the bank,
She made their knees go weak.

Their glasses and their pencils
We're all broken, snapped and shattered.
The onlookers stood gobsmacked
All their clothes were torn and tattered!!

Lot Less submerged triumphant,
As the monster hunters ran,
To see if they had camcorders,
unbroken in the van.

By the time they got back to the loch,
Little "Lot Less" was long gone,
But that night back under water
When they turned their tv on.

On every single channel was a drawing of Lot
Less,
All the witnesses told their story (they were
clearly in distress.)
They described a giant Nessie which could
shriek and wail and scream,
They'd never heard of such a monster,
It was like some awful dream

With every camera battered,
none of them had any proof.
And Lot Less grew much bigger
as their lies took over truth.

Very soon they said she had huge horns,
Others said that she breathed fire,
Every single person listening,
called the witnesses a liar.

But next weekend a massive crowd came to
Scotland just to see
This marvellous new monster: A Scottish loch
banshee!

Both Nessie and her daughter swam and played
beneath the waves,
Lot Less was feeling huge now as she frolicked
through the caves.

She no longer felt like "Lot Less" she was firmly
number one,
And she knew she still would feel this when the
cameras were all gone!

The Alcoholic and Me

19

Sipping beer at breakfast,
Make "Irish" the tea.
Puking by lunchtime,
The alcoholic and me.

A Christmas Lament

Let me declare my love for you
Delicious Brussels Pate.
But why, oh why, oh why, oh WHY!
Must you make me so fat-e?

Stuck Like A...Something

21

What does one do when the words won't come?
Though you stare,
vacantly,
at the page.

You've searched through your notebooks.
You're left feeling glum,
You've screwed up 12 attempts in a rage.

Online you're encouraged to try "simple rhymin,'"
Is gave that a go,
But I've lost my timin'.

I keep getting unrhymables: Opus! Wolf!
Marathon! Silver! Purple! And "Trulf!"

Now I'm making UP words just to climb out this hole!
A "Trulf" - noun: a useless old remote control.

"Pass the "trulf" cried the mother, it's new batteries we need!"
"No, it's "trulfed" replies child it's a "trulf": guaranteed.

Is this what it comes to? Is this how low I've sunk?
Should I try magic mushrooms? Maybe try getting drunk?

Who am I kidding? This poem has stunk!!
The end, it is over...something that rhymes with "stunk!"

A Night on the Town

I'm stood on the platform, the train's late again,
It's cold, and it's windy, and beginning to rain.
My anger is building, but I try to refrain,
There's no use in complaining, no one will explain.

There's blood on the train floor and sick on the seat,
It looks like a sunrise and smells rather sweet.

I look up; there's a fight near the "Parrot and Grape"
The pub on the corner which is run by an ape!

I was barred once for saying my pint was too dear,
Plus "no trainers, no jeans!" "We don't want your type here!
"The Parrot and Grape is for men without fear!"
The bouncers announced with their foot on my ear.

I spring into a taxi and it pulled through the gears,
The gang and the bouncers both spew out some jeers,
I vow to myself as I hold back the tears
That if I ever get home I won't leave it for years!

And I Haven't The Word

When you stood shivering on the pool side,
With a wobbling bottom lip,
I wanted to leap over the rail and snatch you to my
chest.

To march you away from the water,
Away from those gawking
and your fear of the depths.
The gasps for breath and the starter's gun.

But the "On your marks" inspires you.
And the "Get Set" galvanises
And when the crash of the gun hits the water you have
Gone.

You emerge like a torpedo and your clumsiness is sunk,
You are a dolphin. A catamaran, A wave.
Your arms spin metronomically,
Ripples whipping away from each fusillade kick.
Your tiny head encased in red rubber,
Dips and surges.
Ahead, stroke by incremental stroke.

A somersault, crunching your body up
like you are encased in a womb.
Then a piston, exploding

Powering through the water

back the way you came.
The others are catching.
Ever closer
and you are tiring.

The screams are sonar, bouncing towards you.
You are aching and grasping and clutching at water
Stretching for the wall,
A tip of your finger,
A photo finish.

I don't look if you've won.
I watch your exhausted thumbs up in my direction.
You have just raced against your fears.
Am I proud?

I haven't the word for what I am.

Hold on for the Ride

Since I was a teenager. I've heard crazy voices.
Abusive and quite unremitting.
They'll mention how useless my efforts will be,
They suggest benefits to just quitting.

They wiggle acidic (metaphorical) tongues,
Shout out noises that sound hyper real,
I physically flinch when they mention my death,
But there's respite from this daily ordeal.

See along with the voices,
I'm diagnosed with bi polar,
Which is about as annoying,
as a compacted molar,
One minute I'm lower than an adder's left testi,
Then the very next day I am everyone's besty!

When I'm hyper, my outlook, just totally
changes,
I can bake, I can paint, I give big hugs to
strangers.
There is nothing impossible, I could walk
through a wall,
I have charisma: elan! I'm like Lauren Bacall.

Then without any warning I'm desperate again,
I am wrung out, I'm broken, I am lost and in
pain.
When anyone asks I can't ever explain,
The sun has retreated I'm drowning in rain.

The voices come roaring and squealing
delighted,
Remind me again how I'm clearly shortsighted.
No matters the highs, however long they might
last,
The pleasure is transient: total contrast.

What would I give for a peaceful existence,
A mind which allows me,
A break.
Or some distance.

Ensorcelled

Staring at my TV screen,
Whilst glancing at my phone.
Texting, Insta, Snapchat
Is there anybody home?

My child is on their tablet
Whilst my wife is checking e-mail,
My dog is on its Tinder
Swiping right now with its tail.

I check my heart rate on my watch,
Use bluetooth for my oven.
All under lit by ghostly screens,
It's like a hi tech coven.

I Have Never Understood the Fascination

Star Wars? Billy Joel?
Roundabouts? Whack - a - Mole?
Drum and Bass? The Rolling Stones?
Veganism? Savoury Scones?

Boris Johnson? Each Toy Story?
Edward Sheeran? Any Tory?
Scented loo roll? IPAs?
Harry Kane and Milky Ways?

Lonely Planets? Tiki Toks?
Bloody "Linked In"? Funky Socks?
Pablo Picasso? Freezing Showers?
Elon Musk? Plastic Flowers?

Acid Jazz? Climate Deniers?
Fixie Bikes? Long Nosed Pliers?
Talent Shows? Electric Knife?
Computer Chess and most of Life?

The Bloody One Show? The Hammond Organ?
Heavy Metal? Piers Morgan?
Winterwatch? Bobble Hats?
Parking Tickets? Pissing Cats?

University Challenging.

Watching Mr Paxman
Slur the questions at some kids.
About maps or Fibonacci
Ancient trees and Hominids.

I realise I'm ignorant
I'm stupid! I. Am. Dense.
They know the latin ablatives,
I can't define a "fence."

They smash the picture bonuses,
Identify some mountains,
Then name check Gary Lineker
And ancient Roman Fountains.

They know their Asian Rivers,
and the Dutch name for a fox,
Differential calculus
The Greek for "Chicken Pox".

These bleeding lamo students!
They should go and get a job!
Leave me to my ignorance,
A gameshow watching slob!

Our Little Flat

Out little flat.
A place of love and tears.
A palace, a sanctuary, a castle.
There's not enough room to spin a mouse,
but our cat likes it.

I wanted a dog but you won me over,
Like you do with most things.
The decor, the curtains, THAT rug.
Which I thought would be a disaster,
but which you said,
"Would unite the room."

Whatever that means.

It's grown on me though.
Like most of the things you do,
And I wouldn't swap this place for a ranch.
Keep your estates and your gardens.

I'll keep the rug
And the cat
And you.